MUFFIN PLAYS OUTSIDE

by Deborah Sweaney
illustrated by Sally Schaedler

Created and written by Deborah Sweaney.
ilustrated and designed by Sally Schaedler
ISBN: 978-0-578-39094-9

This book is dedicated to first graders, especially those at Mt. Holly Springs Elementary School. You gave me so much joy.   D.S.

With love to my dear children, grandchildren and new grand-baby. S.S.

Muffin was little and black and had a pink tongue. She lived in a brick house with her parents. She had a very good life. She got everything she wanted. She had treats and lots of toys.

There was only one problem.

She could not go outside without
a leash. She watched the other
animals from a window in her
house. They had so much fun.

None of these
animals
had a leash.

Only Muffin.
It was not fair.

One day her parents
accidentally left the door
open a small crack.
Muffin stuck her face
through the crack
and then her whole body.

In a flash she was outside all by herself!
There was no leash holding her back.

A squirrel was gathering acorns by the big oak tree in her yard. Muffin ran up to her. Since all animals can speak the same language, Muffin blurted out her deepest wish in animal speak..."Squirrel, do you want to play?" asked Muffin.

"Sure. You will like climbing to the top of the tree. Follow me."

Squirrel quickly
ran up the tree. Muffin
could barely see her
new friend among the
leaves of the tall tree.
Muffin put her paws
on the thick tree trunk.
She did not know
what to do next.

"Sorry, Squirrel. I don't know how to climb a tree."

She needed to find another friend.

Muffin saw a chipmunk
by the side of the house.
The animal was very small.
Muffin thought, *It looks like
one of my toys. She will
want to play with me.*

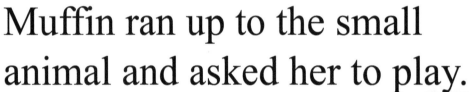

Muffin ran up to the small
animal and asked her to play.

"Of course," said the chipmunk. "I love to play under the bushes." The chipmunk scurried underneath the bushes. She was so fast that Muffin could not follow her.

"Chipmunk, you are too fast."

*I don't know
how to scurry.*

A long-eared bunny sat in a
neighbor's yard. Its tail looked
like a ball of cotton. Muffin said
to herself, "That bunny is just
the right size to play with me."
Muffin ran toward her.

The bunny saw Muffin moving and hopped away. Muffin cried out, "Come back bunny! I just want to play!" It was too late.

The bunny hopped very fast.

Muffin did not know how to hop.

Muffin saw a red breasted robin looking for worms by pecking the ground with its beak. Muffin thought it must be fun to find worms. "Robin, do you want to play?" asked Muffin.
"Sure," said the robin.

"Let's fly over to my favorite tree."

The robin quickly flew away.
Muffin looked up in the sky and saw the robin soaring above her. *How fun it must be to fly,* she thought.

Muffin did not know how to fly.

There was a field on the other side of the tree...

It was surrounded by a fence.

A small goat was eating grass on the other side of the fence.

He is just the right size to play with me, thought Muffin. Muffin ran to the fence and pushed her head underneath it, followed by her body. The goat looked very pleased to see her.

"Let's play, Goat," said Muffin.
The goat shook her head yes. "It is
fun to butt things with your head,"
said the goat.

To Muffin's surprise, the goat placed
her head beside Muffin's rear end
and pushed very hard.

Muffin fell right smack
on the ground,
head first.

"Goat, I don't like the way you play," Muffin said. Muffin did not know how to butt the goat with her head.

Muffin quickly ran back underneath the fence. Her paws moved very fast. She crossed into another field. In the middle of the field, there was a pond. Floating on the blue water were green lily pads.

A large frog sat on the edge of the pond.

"Frog, do you want to play?"
asked Muffin.

"Sure," said the frog. "Let's jump
on the lily pads. It is fun."

The frog took a giant leap
and landed on a lily pad.

Muffin tried to follow,
but she did not know how
to leap. Instead, she
landed right smack
in the water!

Muffin paddled with her paws
and returned to dry land. She
tried to shake off the water,
but she was soaked!

It was time to go home.

Muffin ran and did not stop
until she was at her front door.

Immediately, her parents opened it.
"Muffin, we have been so worried about you. What happened to you? You are all wet."

Muffin's daddy dried her with a towel.
Her Mommy gave her a special treat.

Muffin did not know how to

climb,

scurry,

hop,

fly,

butt, or

leap,

but Muffin knew how to cuddle.

That night, Muffin
curled up in her
mommy's lap. It
was so warm and
nice. She was
very tired after
playing
all day.

She quickly fell
asleep.

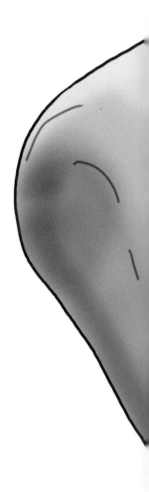

The real Muffin came to live with her people parents, Deborah Sweaney and Jim Baker, when she was seven weeks old. She quickly became an integral member of their family. Muffin's antics form the basis of the *Muffin* stories. This is Deborah's first children's book. Her other books are aimed at an older audience. She was drawn to children's literature after reading to first graders at Mt. Holly Springs Elementary school in Cumberland County, Pennsylvania.

Sally Schaedler brings her years of illustrating children's books to the *Muffin* stories. Her brilliant drawings bring the story to life and capture Muffin's world in colorful images that will delight both children and adults.

CPSIA information can be obtained
at www.ICGtesting.com
Printed in the USA
BVHW021935010722
641068BV00003B/6